GOD'S BIG STORY FOR YOU

GOD'S BIG STORY FOR YOU

Illustrated by Steliyana Doneva

OUR DAILY BREAD
FOR
KIDS
PRESENTS

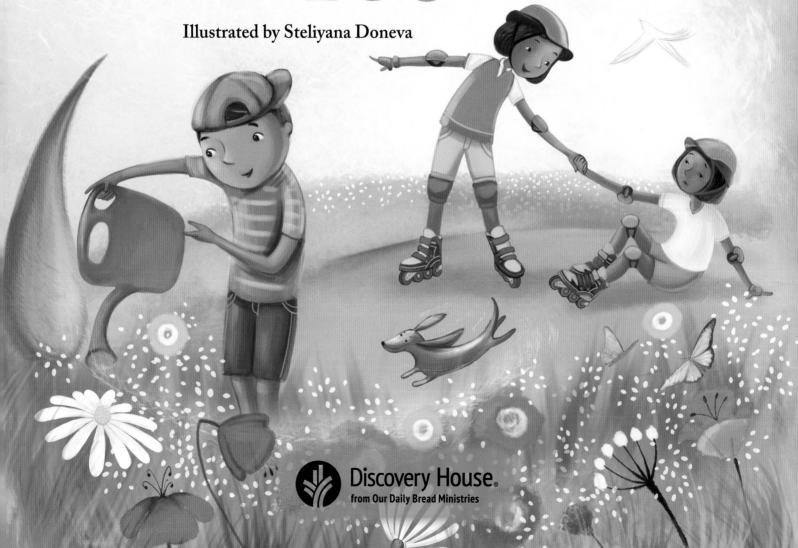

Discovery House
from Our Daily Bread Ministries

GOD'S BIG STORY starts long ago,
before there was you.

4

Before sharks swam in the oceans
 or eagles soared in the sky.
Before there were dinosaurs or trees.
Before the earth and moon were made,
 there was only God.

He was filled with love
and He dreamed of sharing that love.

So God spoke words into the darkness.

let there be light

He created blazing meteors
and colorful sunsets.

Barking puppies
and chomping alligators.

Curious butterflies and velvety roses.
Mountains to scrape the sky and oceans to hug the earth.

But God wasn't done yet.

He made *people* and
put them in a beautiful garden.

Adam and Eve took care of the garden and
everything God had made. They were close to God.
They walked and talked together.
God loved them, and they loved Him.

Until one day . . .

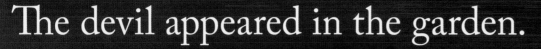

The devil appeared in the garden.

He tricked Adam and Eve and got them to disobey God.

They were ashamed,
so they hid from God.

10

After that,
they weren't close to God anymore.
They had sinned, and sin keeps people away from God.
But God had a plan to send them a Savior,
someone who would rescue them from sin.

Adam and Eve's children and grandchildren
acted the same way. So did all the people after them.
They *all* chose to disobey God.
But God did not stop loving them.

And He did not forget His plan to send a Savior.

God wanted to remind everyone of His love. So He chose a man named Abraham, and promised to make his family into a whole nation. They would be God's people. And their job was really important: to share God's love with the whole world.

God wanted His people to be like a light shining in the darkness, to know His love and share it with others.

I will bless everyone through you

God told Abraham.

Abraham's family would include the Savior,
who would make a way for everyone to return to God.

But sin was ruining everything.

God's people waited. And waited. And waited.

When would their Savior come?

One night, many years later,
a bright star shined over the town of Bethlehem.

God had sent the Savior—Jesus!

Jesus was born to a woman named Mary.
She wrapped Him in strips of cloth
and laid Him in a manger.

Jesus made sick people better, and even brought dead people back to life. He forgave people who had sinned. And He shared God's love with everyone.

But Jesus wasn't done yet.

21

Jesus came to rescue everyone. He came to break the power of sin over the world. To do that, He would have to be separated from God's love, just like Adam and Eve were when they disobeyed God.

Even though Jesus *never* disobeyed God,
He took the punishment for everyone else's sin . . .

23

and on a dark, dark day
He died on a big wooden cross.

Jesus's friends were afraid that God's story was
over, that His promises would never come true,
that they would never know God's love again.

But God wasn't done yet.

Three days later Jesus's friends went
to the place where He was buried. It was empty!

Jesus was alive again!

Jesus had traded His perfect life for our sinful lives
so we could be pure in God's eyes. He destroyed
the power of sin that keeps us away from God.

Jesus returned to His friends. He promised to send them
a helper, the Holy Spirit. The Holy Spirit would comfort
them and remind them that God is always with His people.
Then Jesus told them to share His story with others—

28

God's big story
of love for everyone!

BEFORE THERE WAS YOU, God was filled with love and dreamed of sharing that love.

God created blazing meteors and golden sunsets, curious butterflies and velvety roses.

And God created you,
to enjoy His love and to share His love with others.

That's God's big story for you.

NOTE FOR PARENTS AND TEACHERS

We all need God, and we all have a choice of placing our faith in Him or in ourselves. True hope can only come from trusting in Jesus, and this change of heart comes through God's grace. Encourage your child to believe in the story of God and to trust in the love of God, through Jesus, deep in his or her heart.

A SHORT GLOSSARY

DEVIL: The devil is an evil spiritual being who wants to separate people from God. The Bible calls him "the father of lies" (John 8:44). People who trust Jesus have the power to resist the devil and be close to God.

GOD'S PEOPLE: In the beginning of God's big story, God's people are the nation of Israel. Much of the Old Testament is about this group of people. When Jesus came He said that anybody could be part of God's people! Today, anyone—from any nation—who believes the story of Jesus is part of God's people.

HOLY SPIRIT: The Holy Spirit is the presence of God right here on earth. The Spirit is God's way of being with His people all the time, to offer comfort and to guide. Everyone who believes the story of Jesus has the Holy Spirit with them.

SIN: When people disobey God, they sin. Sin is the opposite of what God wants, and it separates people from God.